The Great Comet of 1996 Foretells

Konstandinos (Dino) Mahoney is based in London, and on the Greek island of Aegina. He won publication of his debut collection, *Tutti Frutti*, in the Sentinel Poetry Book Competition. This is his second collection. Dino teaches Creative Writing at the University of Hong Kong.

First Published in 2022
by Live Canon Poetry Ltd
www.livecanon.co.uk

All rights reserved

© Konstandinos Mahoney 2022

978-1-909703-55-1

The right of Konstandinos Mahoney to be identified as author of this work has been asserted by him in accordance with Section 77 of the Copyright, Design and Patents Act 1988.

A CIP catalogue record for this book is available from the British Library.

For Simon Wu & Athina Dominguez

Acknowledgments

Thanks are due to the editors of the publications in which the following poems appeared:

'The Great Comet of 1996 Foretells' – *Perverse Magazine 5*
'Winter Stasis' – *Shot Glass Journal #36*
'Pastoral' – *Butchers Dog #12*
'Forno' – *erbacce #27*
'Taterdermalion' – *Vers Poetry Competition Collection 2019*
'Intensive Care' and 'Budgie Boy' – *Dempsey &Windle Competition Anthology*
'Hikikomori' – *Live Canon Competition Anthology 2019*
'Helios' – *Mediterranean Poetry 2021*
'Lingua Franca' – *The New European*
'Mâistraki Beach' – *The HighWidow*
'Total Immersion' – *Welsh International Poetry Competition Anthology*
'Her Voice' – *London Grip*
'Twelfth Night' – *Live Canon's New Poems for Christmas*
'Missing The Bongs' – *The New European*

Contents

.

The Great Comet of 1996 Foretells

i

Hong Kong, 3 a.m. – raucous jangling of bells.
He picks up the receiver. A distant voice proclaims,
You are the chosen one! (annunciation).

ii

Kowloon Fertility Unit. He fills in a form, (clay tablet),
receives a semen sample container (silver chalice),
is directed down a corridor (valley) to a WC (natural spring).
Under a neighbouring stall sees lowered jeans crumpled
over size twelve trainers (beast of the field).

iii

Sperm count, motility, morphology normal.
Buys ticket, soars over Ocean of Peace (transmigration).
Transits Los Angeles. Question on immigration form
Reason for entry? Through the airport intercom
a heraldic fanfare of trumpets (proclamation).

Boston Logon. Arrivals. Group embrace with mothers
(trinity), three in one (consubstantial). At home he and
one of the mothers roleplay the coming interview –
in a relationship but separated by work (apocryphal),
why they wish to have a child (revelation).

Cambridge Fertility Clinic. Side by side the couple are
interviewed (judged), approved (find favour).
He fills in a form (clay tablet), is handed a container
(silver chalice), follows a nurse (guardian angel) to a
private room (tabernacle). *Knock twice when you're done.*
Straight porn on the coffee table – *Penthouse, Playboy,*
Debbie Does Dallas (revealed texts). He closes his eyes
(visions). Knocks twice (ritual). Hatch door slides open.

v

Barbeque (burnt offering) with the mothers (trinity).
They drink (communion) to the Great Comet Hyakutake
(holy star), smooth oval head, tadpole tail, streaking bright
over Plum Island (Bethlehem).

Total Immersion

Three days, a continent slips by – Dover, Brussels,
Munich, Belgrade, Athens. Mobbed at the station,
kissed, hugged, pinched, squeezed, Costaki! Costaki!
Καρδιά μου! Χρυσό μου! My Heart! My Golden One!
We drive off like film stars in Pappous' limousine.

He takes me to pavement cafes, watches me scoff
honey cakes, flicks worry beads as he listens to my
anglo-flow, says he's never met a boy who talks so
much, asks mum if he can borrow me, send me to
college, learn Greek.

Baptism day, I stand six years tall in a font for
dunking babies, shy skinny schoolboy in white
underpants. Crammed underwater, I surface to a
slathering of olive oil, taste sunshine, soil,
mum's lettuce salad.

Towel dried, dressed; white shirt, blue shorts,
choir chanting, hearts crossed up down, right left,
right left, Granddad leads me three times round
in circles, then, gold crucifix flashing, out into the
dissolving blaze of the cathedral square.

Athos

Ferry docks in downpour under monastery clinging vertical to Holy Mountain rock.

Monks in furiously flapping rhasons, conical hats, hurry across a rain-lashed gangplank.

Commandeered pilgrims follow with cockerels, fish, eggs, milk, climb a steep stairway.

Relics laid out on trestle tables: Chipped Skull of Stephan the Martyr, Portion of the

Grace Flowing Elbow of Gregory the Theologian, The Precious Zoni of the Theotikos,

The Incorruptible Ear Of Mary Magdalene that every August fills myriad cells with

sacred essence of Eternal Rose so intensely sweet it makes a true believer swoon.

Refectory supper, monastery wine, red cabbage stew, a reading from The Holy Book.

Hand bell clangs. All rise. File out. Glance back regretful at half full bowl and flask.

All night liturgy. Proskynesis, nose tip touches mosaic floor, double-headed eagle,

the globe held tight in its claws. The holy sign of the cross made right left over hearts,

shy flickering icons kissed. Forbidden to sit stand listening to the choir's bass drone,

jingling of the swinging thurible, random clang of caste iron bell lolling in the storm.

Time slows. Geckos of molten wax skitter down the sides of flickering candles.

In white smock, head bowed, curtain of long black glistening hair, a novice waits.

The Hegumenos robed and crowned in Imperial Byzantine gold emerges through

a curtained door in the iconostasis, with ornate silver scissors snips a lock of novice hair.

Released the groom collapses, Christ The Pantokrator looks down from the dome.

At the altar, chalice raised in both hands, a quivering incantation of oriental longing.

Wind howls, sky cracks, wine thickens, bread bleeds.

Mother Olive

Three hundred years she's fruited in this grove, two daughters risen
either side her shallow sprawling roots. She remembers their early years
as only mothers can, in slow, sure rings, slender trunks stretching upwards,
the autumn their first firm green drupes were shaken from their crowns.

She is a ruined castle now, a hollow keep, an open window in her gnarled spine
framing sky, her knotty bark, dribbled candle wax. Her daughters cannot leave,
they will stay until the end, patient nurses at her side. When finally she sinks
back into the soil, they will face each other silent across the void.

Måistraki Beach

Near a little white chapel on the rocks by the sea we sit at
a taverna knocking back ouzo, the trellised vine above us
shivering like a Roma tambourine.

The Gulf churns, mountains of Arcadia mass – Storm Zorba's
on its way. We order another bottle, half fill glasses, add water,
toast the approaching cataclysm with cloudy lion's milk.

Three bottles down we're riffing on death, how to dodge it,
review friends' drinking habits, speculate on the state of their
livers. Fates, we deal out life spans. Order another bottle.

When the blue's rubbed out of a blue world, what's left?
The bleached canvas of beach umbrellas, pale-skinned pebbles,
tabula rasa of an alcohol-rinsed mind.

Forno

A wrong turning leads me to this
forgotten corner, parade of empty shops,
faded signs, bare shelves behind dirty
windows. I park outside the only open
store, step out into drilling sunlight, skirt
an overheated dog collapsed in shade.

At the counter with cold mineral water
the shopkeeper says, *There's bread*,
disappears, comes back with a crusty loaf.
I touch its warm cheek, smile, nod.
She swaddles it in rustling tissue paper,
presents it with a midwife's honest hands.

Winter Stasis

On a clover-covered slope above a cove,

       among silver olives, green Aleppo pines,

a naked fig tree, sap slowed, stark against

       a white winter sky,

lichen blotched trunk,

       matrix of boughs and twigs,

a criss-cross crown, neural circuit,

       floating brain dreaming me, a figment

leaning sideways on a walking stick,

       paused

       in empathetic vacancy.

Triton's Kiss

Clothes abandoned on the sand
with scything arms he powers out to sea,
the sacred isle of Euboea.

His stroke breaks on a dolphin's grinning snout.
Clicking, the mammal buffs against his skin,
slaps him with a playful tail,

spirals down into the deep, rises up with streaming
algae hair, thrusts jelly breasts against his chest,
slips an eel tongue in his mouth,

corkscrews down into the deep, rises with
a bearded grin, barnacled cerulean skin,
gorges on his seafood lips, binds him in a

Triton's kiss.

Helios

At night you can hear things grow — trees, goats, boys.

He wakes up longer than he was the night before,
bony feet jutting up at the end of the bed.

In the bathroom mirror a curious stranger
explores his naked body.

Summer heat builds.
School closes.

Boys backflip off rocks,
sprawl under pines,

above a rumpus of cicadas
tell lies about the girls they've kissed.

One night, in a dark cove
he rubs against a friendly fisherman,

bursts into seed,
collapses into dust.

Heat subsides, school reopens.
He returns to the classroom,

bronzed hirsute legs
splayed either side a shrunken desk.

Pastoral

Pulls over. Parks. Steps out.
Earth touches the soles of his Yeezys,
wind worries his waxed spikes.

Back turned on panorama –
rolling fields, Cheviots, wide blue sky,
takes selfies on his Galaxy –

duck face, fish face, kissy, pouty, smize,
with flicky thumb reviews, checks, selects,
edits, lightens, tightens, tags, types,

All we have is now, and shares. 'Likes'
start coming in, wows, hearts, comments
– *Amazing! Stunning! Lucky you!*

Hermes in Heaven

Kneeling, he snorts
a line of confidence,
muffled music
throbbing overhead,
sniffing, exits the stall,
pinches frosted nostrils,
inspects mirror for proof
of desirability, checks
hairline, sucks in belly,
spies a hunk in hot pants
pissing at the urinal,
bubble butt, rugby thighs,
gold-winged skechers.
The buff god turns –
atomic flash, cisterns flush,
hand dryers roar, taps gush,
soap dispensers foam.
Rigid he rises,
thrusting through the ceiling
onto Heaven's heaving
dance floor.

Goth

In chain store clothes
we eye their raven glamour –
blu-black side-spiked hair,
kohl eyes, matt black lips,
steampunk coat, vegan boots –
pale courtier of darkness
enthroned on Central Line
moquette, hurtling towards
Mile End.

Buzz cut, polo shirt,
Nike trackies, fit bloke
boards, sits opposite.
Doors slide shut.
He leans forward, says,
Fucking freak. We stare
at screens, out windows,
up at ads, read Poem on
the Underground.

Rules of Courtship

He yanks them up, not noticing
they've faded, behind their shrivelled
heads he sees the perfect bloom.

He offers his bouquet to a passing girl.
She quickens her step, not running
as running only makes things worse.

He hurries after, pleading – he's been
inside so long he's forgotten how things
are done, and he's skipped his medication.

Police car arrives, an ambulance takes him
off. Scattered in the road, a mangled bunch
of dead daffodils.

Cut Flowers

Hot humid afternoon, toxic canyon,
trapped diesel fumes.

He steps into a flower shop,
chilled sanctuary, floral mortuary,

hectic blooms on severed stems,
mist-sprayed elegance on count down.

He waggles before pouting pinks,
orange bugles on stiff wands,

golden nebulae, anemones
blue as drowned lips.

Scorpion Grass

Everything his lover left behind, books, clothes,
gets bagged, binned, donated to Oxfam.

In a window box, shoots appear, froth into
sky-blue, yellow-throated clusters,

the forget-me-nots he planted last year,
seeds bought at the garden centre.

Too pretty to uproot,
a daily stay of execution.

Falling Man

(Giacometti 1950)

This brass
  bean-pole's
    attenuated body
    silhouetted
   against vacant
    space at the
      tipping tripping
        point between
        upright and flat
          on his face
          bony big toe
          stubbed on a
          rock heels risen
          teetering toppling
                alone
                nothing to
                cling to head
                      yanked back
                      arm sprung out
                      survival reflex
                      leaning too far
                      forward to
                      reverse
                  natural law
                decrees a fall
              gravity the gorilla
              on his back
          face far from
     feet walking
     head in the
     clouds
     how
       distant the
          pavement seems
          until unbalanced
          he's brought
          down to earth.
        Looked at from
            different angles
        he's riding a horse dancing
        arms akimbo diving long
        and naked into a clear Swiss lake.

Budgie Boy

In a frantic flutter of wings he springs from the opened cage door,
flies up to the kitchen washing line, hangs upside down, swallow dives,
lands on my shoulder, nibbles the juicy jungle fruit of my fleshy ear lobe.

Perched on my index finger, he is my first kiss, pecking my lips, his little
beak tasting of millet and cuttlefish. Every day we chirp to each other,
blink in avian Morse, close as bird and boy could ever be.

How did it happen, the separation? Those little acts of cruelty? His injured
wing? When, occasionally, I remembered him, my pimpled face looming at
the bars, he'd turn his back, gaze in the mirror as if I wasn't there.

Working from Home (8):
Anaconda

Dinner's ready! There's
usually a stampede.
Where are they? Jake's
not in his room, and
when I check on Andy
he's sprawled out on
the bedroom floor. I
totally lose it, think
he's had a heart attack.
Then I see his belly –
huge. And he's
smiling.

I'd been working on
this spreadsheet all day
– my biggest client.
Jake creeps in, roars
right in my ear and
poof, whole thing
vanishes.
I'm a lion, what are you?
An anaconda.
What's that?
A big snake that can
swallow little boys.
Next thing I know
I'm flat out on the
floor, Trish is
screaming.

I asked Daddy what
animal he is,
A BIG SNAKE and I can
swallow you!
I'm TOO BIG to
swallow! And he said,
he said,
I can unlock my jaws.

Intensive Care

Buzzing bump bumps
against the skylight.

He fetches the steps, makes a shaky ascent,
reaches for the cobwebbed handle.

It waggles about his outstretched fingers.
Bee or wasp? Does it matter?

For everything living is holy
he looks down at tonight's dinner,

lamb chops defrosting on the draining board.
He gives up, descends.

Morning. In the glossy white ceramic sink,
a fleck of tiger fur.

He nudges it onto a water bill,
carries it out into the back yard,

tips the patient gently into intensive care –
a cat-sprayed patch of peppermint.

Doppelgänger

Zigzags through the crowded foyer
eager look on his young handsome face,
stops in front of me, smiling, I smile back,
relishing the misdirected sunshine.

Sorry, but I had to come over, you see,
you look exactly like my father, clothes,
hair, everything. When I speak he shakes
his head, amazed — *Your voice too, identical.*

And his father's a musician, viola not violin —
but strings! A woman beckons. Time to go.
He squeezes my hand, hugs me, holds me,
I inhale his lemon cologne.

Walk to the underground, no umbrella,
cold, drenching rain, but inside I'm glowing,
knowing for the first time the full force
of a child's love.

Deschooling Society

A major illusion on which the school system rests is that most learning is the result of teaching (Ivan Illich)

They take their classes to the local waterways – *Write a poem about canals.* The kids drift off in search of shade. Teachers make their escape, Sir behind Sir, on a Yamaha.

They drink beer on a bench in Soho Square, loll together in a darkened Odeon, grope for salty popcorn in a shared jumbo carton.

Next day they check their students' work –
The canals were too straight to write about, Sir.

Manhattan Dialogues

Cabbie won't stop outside the Y, drops us a safe distance away, we pay through a bulletproof screen. At the entrance a hawker pushes CDs. We ask about the music – *I don't listen to this shit man.*

Check in, busted lock, bare cell, bunk beds. At a local bar we suck bourbon on the rocks through short plastic straws. On the way back get hassled for cash. We ask if he takes sterling. He runs away.

Dawn. Friend rings, *Leave now while you can.* We sneak out, grab a cab, spend the day at her West Side brownstone learning how to lock, bolt, chain her apartment door – stepfather's just got out of jail.

We check into the Chelsea. Something plunges past our window. On 14th a hooker grabs me, won't let go. I tell her we're on our way to Christopher Street, *Honey*, she says, *I am Christopher Street.*

Acid House

Blotting paper micro dots
on poked out tongues.

Fridge purrs, clock ticks.
He shrugs, walks her home.

Streets turn canvas flats,
a zombie's arm juts out a pillar box.

Refuge in a bedsit.
All night he reads a shaving mirror,

rotates its silver pages,
the revolving book of him.

Bolt upright on a wooden chair
she prepares for fiery martyrdom,

spends next day soaking in a tub -
he sits at table staring at his face

upside down in a spoon.

Papa Voodoo

Fetch string, straw,
his old brown boiler suit,
working boots, a hollow
pumpkin head, shake
a baccy tin of tacks,
sprinkle *eau de vie*,
blow till you're giddy,
till his limbs get twitchy,
then zip up your stab vest
and scarper, the dead can get
frisky.

He leaps up, mouth
bristling with nails,
measures me shoulder
to shoulder, tip to toe,
lines up the spirit level's
glaucous eye, draws pencil
crosses on planks of wood,
saws, glues, hammers,
lifts me, lays me, tucks
me in, kisses my eyes, fits
the lid, lowers the casket.

Mother Hen

Cackling she comes, nests on my face,
lays an egg in my mouth.
I feather over, sprout a gristle comb.

Wake, belly pod crisscrossed with scratches.
Queasy pong of man-sweat, damp socks,
jogging gear. I chew on a lemon.

Showered he comes, the cock that laid me,
briefcase, suit and tie, pecks my cheek,
struts off to work proud, pigeon-toed.

Momotaro

A plump peach comes bobbing down
a mountain stream.

An old hunter wades in, scoops it out.
The fruit throbs in his hand.

He puts it to his ear, hears ticking.
Cuts it open with a paring knife.

Curled in its crimson hollow,
a tiny babe.

He spills it into his cupped palm,
blows it dry.

Tiny cries unlock his heart.
Blessed, he eats the afterbirth,

wraps his tot in a maple leaf,
takes her home.

Hikikomori *

My first sight of him —
a sonogram

bald swollen head
fused eyes

foetal alien
attached to a feeding cord.

I climb the stairs. Tap
twice. Withdraw.

A pale hand slides in
the tray.

Tethered to his earphones
I do not hear the gunfire,

screams, moans, music
downloading into him.

I look up when the toilet flushes,
reassured.

Reclusive adolescent withdrawn from social life

No Subtitles

Gavel cracks, baby plucked from mother,
delivered to father. The infant frees a
swaddled arm, brandishes a tiny fist.
Close up of mother's anguished face.
Soundtrack of weeping violins.

Commercial break, catchy Urdu jingles.
I grab a *Murree* from the hotel mini bar.
What had she done, the mother in the dock? What had
I done, my son taken from me back in Birmingham?

She's staring at an empty cot, is injected
with a silver needle – eyes roll, head lolls.
Strings spiral down a wormhole of oblivion.
In my group, some fathers went that way,
pain neutered with opiode amnesia.

She's on a roof. Unpegging baby clothes
she spots a plane, delirious, bursts into
high-pitched song. Uprush of ecstatic violins.
As the jet roars over she raises loving arms –
and I raise mine.

Peace Pipe

Now! she goes. He sucks hard, the bowl seethes, smoke shoots up the stem, down his throat, fills his lungs. He tries hard to hold it in, coughs, chokes it out in racking spasms. She laughs. What's he like?

He hopes this will bring them together, sharing a smoke, having a laugh. Out the window he sees people queuing at a bus stop in the rain. He counts them – five, six, seven – the years they've been apart.

He asks what she remembers. *A film you made me watch when I was six, a man gets eaten by ants, everything except his glasses.*

Chimp

He dreads her acts of charity, like that time in Bali,
a chimp smuggled into their room.
He clings to her, hairy mite, velvet waistcoat,
soft brown eyes, she kisses his head,
gives him a name, laughs when he pulls her hair,
climbs the curtains, pees on the bed, *He's marked
his place*, she says. Jolted awake by shattered glass,
she pleads with him to spare her duty free.
He lobs a bottle of *Eternity*. Shown the door
he scampers off, leaves behind a pong of perfume
laced with poo. Next day he's back at reception,
chained. At checkout she fills in the feedback form –
Animals are human too, you know.

Lesbos

He scans the horizon –
no sign of a ferry.
Choppy seas,
the *meltemi* is strong today.
He upends his flitzani,
twists it three times
on its saucer the way
yia-yia used to do.
She could read coffee cups,
see the future in muddy
pictograms. A boy at her side
he'd listen as she told his
aunties what was in store
for them. *Never do your own,*
she warned him.
He peers into his demitasse,
the dribbled glyphs,
sees a capsized boat,
stickmen, arms raised,
floundering in the sea.
A blast of hot wind,
his napkin flies away,
plastic water bottle
clatters to the ground.
He pays, leaves.
New notice outside
the ticket office –
All ferries cancelled.
He rents a room above a bakery.

From the street below,
women's voices —
Παναγία, Holy Virgin.
Must have put them in a sieve.
Their mothers' wombs
will rip a second time.

Circus Act

Garish poster tied around a tree, they see
a cat on fire, ashen uncle with bloody lips,
kidnapped sisters in a warlord's arms.

Circus, a local tells the wide-eyed refugees,
mimes a tiger leaping through flames, a clown,
girls standing on a strongman's outstretched arms.

The show was a dud, starving llama, drunken clown,
a flabby strongman, body gone to seed. Benches empty,
wages unpaid, they packed up, went their separate ways.

Gone now, he sighs shaking his head. *But if you hurry,*
he adds enthusiastically, fingers scampering down
an imaginary road, *you can catch them up.*

Tatterdemalion

Beaks open like squeezed clothes pegs
cawing crows perch on his outstretched arms
take turns to tug nesting from his head.

The weathered thread that binds him breaks,
he slumps to earth, crawls through corn,
stands up and staggers down the tractor's way,

comes to an inn smothered in ivy, a painted sign
hanging on a pole, a flying blue goat, gold-feathered
wings.

Locals eye him as he enters, flops boneless against
the counter. Landlord pulls a pint of flat. Thirsty,
he empties it over his head.

Smelling sport, they flock. *Where you from Bendy Man?*
Where you park your caravan? Buy us a drink, will you?
Lend us a fiver.

He runs away upstairs, out window, up pipe, on roof,
looks down at upturned faces, over at yellow fields.
The song that must be sung rises in him.

His stitched-up mouth snaps open, he bawls out his
ballad, the scarecrow who rides the skies on the back
of a blue goat with golden wings.

Jump! a wag shouts up at him, *Jump! Jump!* they chant
banging bucket and dustbin lid, holding out their arms
as if to catch him.

Uprising

Outside a Hong Kong shopping mall,
amplified bursts of recorded birdsong
from artificial trees.

Next morning, on the pavement,
lungs scorched with last night's dioxin –
dead starlings.

Lingua Franca

1948

The bus conductor clips their tickets.
They chatter as they cross Hammersmith Bridge
en route to the Lyons factory.

They married Tommies, went back with them to
bombed out neighbourhoods, ration books, queues,
curious families.

Speak English! a voice behind them booms,
This is England! an angry man explains
to the Athenian brides.

They ring the bell, apologetic ting,
get off, walk to work, are late
clocking in.

2018

Train's packed, she's hanging on a strap, chatting to
her mother on her phone,
No te preoccupies, everything's fine,

I'm sharing with some other nurses, sometimes we
cook together —
adobo, fasolakia, paella.

This is England! Speak English!
Por qué me gritas? flustered, she answers
in her mother tongue.

He punches her, escapes through open doors.
Passengers gawp, it happened so fast,
what could they do?

Bayonet

Zeppelin clouds barrel across a riled-up sea.
They huddle together on Dunkirk sands,

stories snatched from their lips by sudden squalls,
how their dad's best mate lost his head,

blasted through the air, *like a football,* he said,
how he waded out to *The Hilda*, a Dutch coaster.

And granddad at the Somme, up to his chin in mud,
could never breath properly again,

and how at night, when they were kids,
his bayonet made scary sounds in the wardrobe,

rasping as if fighting for breath.

Sandy

Putney Vale, wide rolling fields of white headstones.
One of them is Sandy Denny's.

I saw her once, a distant figure on a stage
performing just for me.

I google it – Block 5, Plot 38.
A talking map guides me to a modest plot,

The Lady, 1947–78 -
a heart-shaped balloon grazes on green stones.

I play her greatest hits on Spotify,
ear bud intimacy, remastered clarity,

singing to me from beyond the grave.

Awakenings

Asleep on a beach,
        clack of copper bell,
rancid whiff of curd.
        Eyes open on a bearded goat,
sun lodged between his horns,
        grazing on my hairy chest.

Face down in an olive grove,
        felled by wine.
A triumph of ants marches past my nose
        dragging with them
a mighty horn-helmeted stag beetle,
        captive Gothic war lord.

Trucks thunder past in the rain throwing up
        arched wings of spray.
On a grassy patch by the autobahn,
        cocooned in a damp sleeping bag,
I wake with a snail on my lips –
        Charon's obol.

Her Voice

She said to one she'd come back in her dreams,
to the other, in music, to me, as a voice – she sounded so certain,
propped up against firm hospital pillows, talking between
teaspoons of apricot yogurt she later threw up.

As a boy, I once made a crystal set – plywood, wire, foil,
summoned voices from thin air talking in foreign tongues.
Now, through the static whine of tinnitus, I listen for her
voice, a message from a foreign station, a distant star.

Did You Write This?

She materializes in the steamed up
bathroom mirror brandishing a book.
I recognize the garish cover.
Did you write this? she asks, voice
quivering with distress.
I lower my toothbrush,
It doesn't mean I didn't love you,
I say, mouth
foaming with toothpaste.
There's a loud metal crack.
Ouch! A mouse expires.
At least that was quick,
she snaps, *this book
could last forever!*
I feel a guilty surge of pride.
Why did you write it? Why?
I search for an answer.
Mothers are important.
I was trying to understand.
It's not enough. She gives me
a hurt, Medusa stare.
Evaporates.
I rinse my mouth, dry my hair,
put on clean shorts, t-shirt,
empty the mousetrap,
drink milk, get into bed,
turn off the light,
sink into sleep
where she's waiting for me
in the underworld with
the same frightened eyes
she fixed on me
the morning she died.

Twelfth Night

Peg-legged, balding, bare,
dumped outside as whining vacuums
suck up fallen needles.

Those that threw them out
first waltzed them in,
dressed them in jewels,

draped them in pulsing lights,
crowned them with stars,
stacked gifts at their feet

and with shut eyes inhaled
the resin scent of fairy tale,
dull brick morphing into

gingerbread. Now, back to work,
owners look the other way,
embarrassed by the line

of amputees abandoned on
the pavements, tawdry lametta
clinging to their branches,

ashamed of the child that
took them in, the adult
that turfed them out.

Missing The Bongs

Tonight, as we leave the Globe, the deep dark
Thames surges single-minded under the Millennial Bridge,
merciless if you fall in, your ferry collides. It's in no
mood to pose for a photo, just wants to flow the hell back

out to sea away from this lunacy. Somewhere across the
water a terrified bird is squealing, the sound pigs make in
an abattoir. It is the night of leaving when those in favour
would have us celebrate, a Tyburn carnival, ale and pies as

bodies dangle. People pass, heads bowed against the rain,
voices snatched by the wind. A busker in the tunnel tucks
his violin tenderly into its battered case, closes the lid –
he's going home, though he's no longer sure where that is.

Waterloo station, hushed cathedral ready for a requiem.
A red-faced reveller fresh off a train, wrapped in a nylon
union flag, is on his way to Parliament Square, and he has
to be quick, he doesn't want to miss the bongs.